AF270404

Understanding Deepfakes

JENNIFER SANDERSON

CHERITON
CHILDREN'S BOOKS

Published in 2026 by **Cheriton Children's Books**
1 Bank Drive West, Shrewsbury, Shropshire, SY3 9DJ, UK

© Copyright 2026 Cheriton Children's Books

First Edition

Author: Jennifer Sanderson
Designer: Paul Myerscough
Editor: Kelly Short
Proofreader: Amy Strauss

Picture credits: Cover: Shutterstock/GaudiLab. Inside: p4: Shutterstock/Fizkes, p5: Wikimedia Commons/MidJourney AI, p6: Shutterstock/Markus Photo and Video, p7: Shutterstock/MDV Edwards, p8: Wikimedia Commons/Edward Webb, p9: Shutterstock/AI Generator, p11: Shutterstock/Tero Vesalainen, p13: Shutterstock/Xavier Lorenzo, p14: Shutterstock/Anton Ivanov, p15: Shutterstock/Roman Zaiets, p16: Shutterstock/Kaspars Grinvalds, p17: Shutterstock/Antonio Guillem, p18: Shutterstock/Africa Studio, p19: Shutterstock/Carballo, p20: Shutterstock/Pranithan Chorruangsak, p21: Shutterstock/Ivan Cholakov, p23: Shutterstock/Goodluz, p24: Shutterstock/Igor Link, p25: Wikimedia Commons/MidJourney AI, p26: Shutterstock/DC Studio, p27: Shutterstock/McLittle Stock, p28: Shutterstock/Alessia Pierdomenico, p29: Wikimedia Commons/Stable Diffusion, p30: Shutterstock/PeopleImages.com/Yuri A, p31: Shutterstock/Pics Five, p33: Shutterstock/Dean Drobot, p34: Shutterstock/Song about Summer, p35: Shutterstock/YanLev Alexey Sizov, p36: Shutterstock/Kaspars Grinvalds, p37: Shutterstock/Khorzhevska, p38: Shutterstock/Monkey Business Images, p39: Shutterstock/Pixel Shot, p40: Shutterstock/Tapati Rinchumrus, p41: Shutterstock/Summit Art Creations, p43: Shutterstock/Jose Calsina, p44: Shutterstock/Daniel Hoz, p45: Shutterstock/Ollyy.

Printed in China

Please visit our website,
www.cheritonchildrensbooks.com
to see more of our high-quality books.

Contents

Teens Go Online

In 2024, 96 percent of teenagers said they use the Internet daily. When spending so much time online, it's important to know how to keep yourself safe.

Being a teenager means change, and a lot of it! At this time of life, you are changing from a child into a young adult. Physical changes aside, you're also learning the skills to help you as an adult, from being more independent and making decisions to figuring out your values. You are also trying to find your place in the world—and that includes finding your place in the online world.

The Online World

In 1989, English computer scientist Sir Tim Berners-Lee invented the World Wide Web (WWW). The Web is an information system found on the Internet that allows people to find and share information and to communicate. Originally, the Web was built to help scientists share research. It has since grown so much that in 2025, there were 5.56 billion Internet users around the world, all surfing the Web.

When It's Good, It's Great

The Internet and the World Wide Web can be great. People around the world use the Web for learning. School, universities, and other educational institutions publish material online. People can also read books online or watch movies. Social media has also changed how relationships work. Using the Internet, people can interact with other users on the other side of the world at the click of a button. They can send them messages, emails, and play games with them.

Often fake images, like this one, are easy to spot. However, deepfakes can be very believable.

When It's Bad, It's Damaging

While the Internet and Web are incredible tools, if not used correctly, they can be harmful. With billions of websites, the Web can be very distracting. It is easy to waste a lot of time on it, just surfing the Web almost for the sake of it. That is not healthy for our minds. Social media in particular can also lead to mental health problems such as anxiety and depression. And then there are crimes carried out online that result in the loss of personal data and the spreading of dangerous and misleading information.

Deepfake Danger

One way to spread false information is by creating deepfakes. A deepfake is a fraudulent image, audio clip, or video that is made using artificial intelligence (AI). This book is going to help you understand deepfakes. By the end of it, you'll know what they are and how to spot them. You'll understand why they are dangerous and how to protect yourself from them. Keep a look out for the How to Survive Online panels—they'll help you work your way through difficult scenarios that you may face.

Teen Need to Know

A shallowfake is a fake image, video, or document. It is made without AI using a technique known as shallow editing. Sometimes, shallowfakes are also called cheapfakes. They are made by editing, or changing, content using simple software.

CHAPTER 1

What Is a Deepfake?

In the late 1980s, the first digital photos appeared. Instead of using film, these photos were stored on a memory card in the camera. The files were then transferred to a computer. Then, in 1990, when more people started owning digital cameras, the first version of Adobe Photoshop was launched. Using Photoshop, people could edit their digital images. For example, it was easy to remove a zit on a chin or change an image from color to black and white. While quite simple by today's standards, these photo edits began the process of creating shallowfakes. Deepfakes take this idea of editing images one step further and create something completely new.

Fakes That Run Really Deep

Deepfakes differ from shallowfakes in that to create the fake image, a special type of AI known as deep learning is used. Deep learning trains computers to act like the human brain. The computers can process data so that they recognize patterns in not only images but text, sounds, and other information too. The computers use those patterns to produce insights and predictions. In the past, only smart tech specialists could create deepfakes.

Digital cameras allowed photographers to immediately see their photo without needing to wait to have it processed in a laboratory. And afterward, using software like Photoshop, they could edit the image to perfect it.

Face swapping is just one of the ways content creators use AI to create deepfakes.

Today, the tech needed to create a deepfake is available to everyone with an Internet connection. You don't need any specialist knowledge. All you need are clear images, an app, an Internet connection, and time on your hands.

Some Deepfake History

The first deepfakes came about in 2017. A Reddit user with the username "deepfakes" shared doctored videos. He used Google's open source, deep-learning technology to swap celebrities' faces onto the bodies of adult entertainers to create new, fake images. Open source technology is tech that is freely available. It is developed and available for anyone to use, change, and share again and again, as much as they like.

Since the first deepfake was posted, the number of deepfakes has rocketed by 550 percent! In 2023, there were nearly 96,000 recorded deepfake videos. With so many deepfakes out there, it's really important that you understand how they are made and how to spot them, so keep reading.

Today's Deepfakes

Today, as well as face swapping, the creators of deepfakes use voice cloning. In voice cloning, AI is used to mimic, or copy, a person's voice. The voice can say anything the creator wants it to. Deepfakes can also use lip syncing. This is when a person's lips move in time to a voice recording, so it seems that they are speaking the words. Sometimes, the audio can be a deepfake so there's an extra layer of deception.

Using deepfake technology, the face at the top has changed into the face at the bottom.

How Tech Makes Deepfakes

When the first deepfake was made, the tech was basic and the fake was not so difficult to spot. Early deepfakes were made using a generative adversarial network (GAN). Today, GANs are still used to create deepfakes. Using a GAN, people can generate, or make, new images from existing digital images and videos. They can also make new songs from existing songs. A GAN uses deep learning to recognize patterns in the existing images, video, or audio. It then uses the patterns to create the fakes. To do this it uses two networks: the generator network and the discriminator network.

The Deepfake Process

The generator network tries to create the fake. It views the image from all angles and analyzes it to find patterns. It then creates the fake digital content. The content is then run through the discriminator network. The discriminator's job is to tell the difference between the real and fake images, video, or audio. When it identifies the content as real or fake, it passes the information back to the generator. The generator fine-tunes the image and sends it back to the discriminator. This process is repeated until the discriminator can no longer tell the fake from the original. This means that each time a deepfake is created, the next one will be even better.

Changing Faces

Another smart way of creating deepfakes uses AI algorithms called autoencoders. They are found in face-replacement and face-swapping technology. In this tech, a person runs thousands of shots of two faces through an autoencoder called the encoder. The encoder finds and learns similarities between the two faces. It then reduces them to their shared common features. The data that is left is called the compressed data.

A second autoencoder, a decoder, is taught to recover the compressed data—in this case, the faces from the images. Because the faces are different, the decoder is trained to recover the first face. Another decoder is taught to recover the second person's face. To swap the images, the person creating the deepfake feeds the images into the wrong autoencoder. The decoder retrieves and swaps the images of faces, allowing a face to be superimposed on another person's body.

Teen Need to Know

In 2023, on a cold morning, the former head of the Catholic Church, Pope Francis, went outside St Peter's Basilica in Vatican City, Italy. There, he greeted faithful Catholics. When images of this event were published, people couldn't help but notice that the pope was wearing a white puffer jacket. The images (similar to the one below) went viral. However, it was soon discovered that they were fake! They were made using specialist AI software called Midjourney.

Midjourney is an art generator—you type in what you want to see, and with the click of a tab, the image appears. No specialist knowledge is needed, just Internet access. As time goes on, more sites like Midjourney will appear and the technology will keep on improving. That means deepfakes are going to become more sophisticated than ever, and much easier to create.

Close examination of the zip on this jacket will tell you that this image is fake.

Keeping up with the Law

Tech is always changing. That makes it very difficult for the law to keep up. The laws that govern, or control, the Internet are called cyberlaws. Cyberlaws around the world vary, and the laws around deepfakes are different from country to country. In the United States, there are also different laws depending on what state you live in.

Controlling the Deepfake World

Around the world, those who create the software used in deepfakes must follow their country's laws. For example, in China, any new technology is governed by laws that state the tech must not cause harm to the public. Deepfakes must be labeled as such so that fake information is not spread (there'll be more about this later). In the European Union (EU), those who create the software for deepfakes are governed by the EU AI Act. This law states that systems that create or manipulate images, audio, and video must meet certain standards. For example, service providers must tell users when they are interacting with AI systems so that tabs are kept on deepfakes.

Rules for Creators

Those who create deepfakes are governed by laws, too. For example, in Indonesia it's not illegal to create deepfakes. However, using deepfakes to spread false information, create adult content, or defame a person's character is against the law. Some countries such as the United Arab Emirates (UAE) allow shallow edits but have guidelines around using AI to create deepfakes.

A Person's Right to Be Private

Most countries have laws around privacy. Privacy laws are there to protect people's personal information. That includes the use of their name, voice, signature, and photographs or likeness. Most privacy laws state that personal information cannot be shared without the person's consent, which means agreeing to something. By taking a person's image and changing it without their consent, the law is being broken. That applies even if the person is a public figure and their images are everywhere. For example, when AI-generated explicit images of Taylor Swift were posted on X, there were more than 45 million views and more than 20,000 reposts. The fake images caused significant damage to Swift.

When It's Not Good to Share

Manipulating images of people and then sharing them can seem like fun. However, you cannot take a person's likeness and use it and/or share it without their permission. If someone asks you to help create a fake image of another person (for example, a teacher), always say no. There are serious consequences to that action:

- Once the image is created, and circulated online, there is no way to take it back.
- You could deeply upset the person whose image you have used. Think about how you'd feel if someone did that to you.
- You might find yourself in trouble with the law for illegally using a person's image. It is not worth taking that risk.

UNDERSTANDING DEEPFAKES

You now know what deepfakes are. You've discovered the tech used to make them, and the laws that govern their use. That means you are a step closer to navigating deepfakes in the digital world. Here's a recap of what we've discovered so far.

1 Shallowfakes Are Everywhere

Shallowfakes or cheapfakes are made using simple editing software and techniques. There is no AI involved.

2 Deepfakes Are Made Using Complex AI

AI technology that enables deep learning is used to make deepfakes. In today's fast-paced digital world, you don't need a lot of specialist computer knowledge. You just need the Internet, some images, video, audio, and time.

3 There Are Laws to Protect You

While there are no blanket laws against deepfakes, many countries have specific laws and guidelines that govern their use.

4 Privacy Is Key

Most countries have laws to protect people's privacy. No one can take your image or likeness and use it without your consent.

Tech Changes All the Time

Technology seems to always be advancing. Just when you think you are on top of it, a new idea comes along and changes everything! But remember, just because everyone is embracing new tech, you don't have to. Try being a "late adopter" and see how the tech plays out before you hop on board.

CHAPTER 2

The Good and the Bad

Like most things in life, there are pros and cons to deepfakes. The tech used to create deepfakes is amazingly smart and how it's used can be incredible. However, it can also cause many, many problems. Let's look first at the positives.

Deepfakes for Education

One of the smartest uses of deepfakes is in the classroom. Deepfakes can really bring history to life. Instead of listening to a teacher talk about a speech that an important historical figure gave, thanks to deepfakes, you could see and hear that very same speech in your classroom.

Educators can also join forces with AI specialists to create amazing support material for students. Rather than a video lecture for everyone to watch, an AI tutor using deepfake technology can create feedback and learning to suit each student. Even the language of instruction could be different for each student. This makes learning more accessible and effective for everyone.

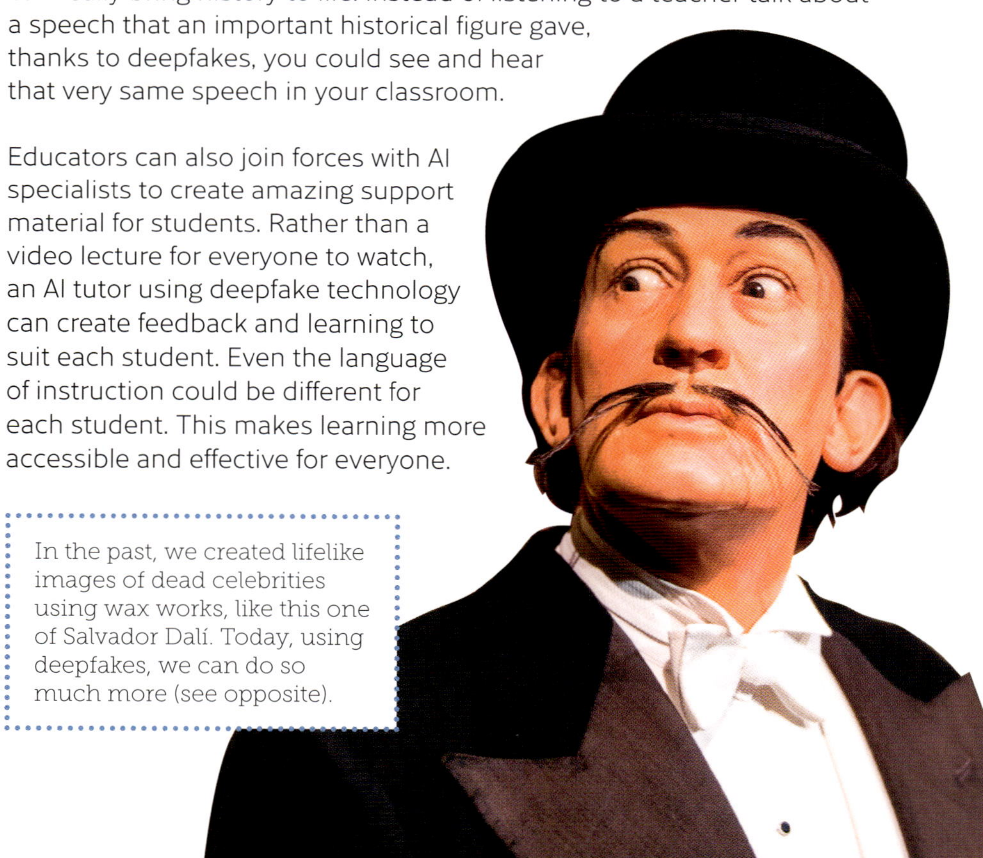

In the past, we created lifelike images of dead celebrities using wax works, like this one of Salvador Dalí. Today, using deepfakes, we can do so much more (see opposite).

Beyond the Classroom

Deepfake use for education can now reach far beyond the classroom. For example, former soccer player David Beckham took part in a campaign to raise awareness about malaria. This is one of the world's deadliest diseases. Using deepfake tech, the audio he provided was translated into different languages to make it seem that Beckham was actually speaking in those languages. This meant the campaign had a greater reach and raised more awareness than if it were only in English.

Deepfake can be used for artistic purposes too. For example, smart tech brought the artist Salvador Dalí to life. In an exhibition called "Dalí Lives" at the Dalí Museum in St Petersburg, Florida, a life-sized video display showed Dalí. He was talking in a voice that was just like his own. He even posed for selfies with visitors!

Deepfakes Saving Lives

Deepfakes can also be used in the medical industry. In hospitals around the world, doctors use special machines called magnetic resonance imaging (MRI) scanners to take pictures of the inside of the body. These pictures help find problems such as tumors. Some tumors, such as cancerous tumors, are dangerous. To help computers learn how to spot tumors in MRI pictures, scientists need a lot of examples. But some types of tumors are rare, and it can be hard to find enough pictures to properly train the computers. With the help of AI, the computer uses the deepfake images—along with real ones—to practice spotting tumors more accurately, helping doctors find unusual problems faster and more easily when scanning real patients.

AI deep learning has helped doctors better detect rare and unusual tumors.

In a survey published in 2024, learners aged 13 to 17 were asked how they used AI. Many students said that they "used it in a good way." For example, they used it to ask for help with papers or to create individualized learning plans. Of the users, 31 percent said they used AI to make pictures or images. Sixteen percent used it to create sounds and music.

Fake news isn't usually labeled as "fake." That makes it difficult to tell what's true and what isn't.

Deepfakes in Entertainment

Deepfakes have been used in the movie industry for some time. For example, if a movie has a flashback of a younger version of a character, deepfakes can be used for this. They can also be used to make characters seem much older. They can take this one step further and even bring a dead actor back to life!

Spreading the News

While deepfakes can be used positively, it's most often the negative uses that feature in the media. And at the top of the list is disinformation, or fake news. All it takes is for someone to create a video and post it online. Once online, people believe the clip is real and share the information. They may believe that they are doing good and passing on valuable news. What they don't realize is that by spreading disinformation, they are creating even bigger problems.

Deepfakes in Politics

Spreading fake news is a daily problem. But that problem is even more serious during an election. The results of elections affect everyone, from the people running for election to the people voting for them. The fake news spread may include information that a polling station is closed. It may show documents that are needed by people in order to vote. It may suggest election tampering took place at a particular station. Election tampering means altering people's votes or the counting and recording of votes.

Vote This Way

Along with spreading fake news, deepfakes can also be used to convince people to vote in a certain way. For example, they may spread false information about a candidate. The US government was so concerned about this that in the run-up to the 2024 election, it created videos warning people not to trust unverified information.

How to Stop the Scam

Stopping and thinking before you react to a message on your phone can help you avoid being caught out by disinformation. For example, a scam might involve you receiving a prerecorded message on your phone saying that your school will shut for the next three days due to a gas leak. Always question such a message before reacting. In this instance, you should:

- Double check the information you've received. Check with your parents and ask them to contact the school to verify the message. You will know immediately if it is fake or real.
- Check with schoolfriends to see if they have received a message too. If they have, it could be a widespread scam. Tell them and their parents to check with the school too. If the school is alerted, staff can tell everyone about the fake news and stop the scam before people take it seriously.

Stealing What's Yours

Identity theft is the stealing of your personal information. That might include your name and Social Security Number, for example. With these details, scammers can open new accounts such as store cards. They can fraudulently use your bank accounts and withdraw money from them.

Deepfake creators usually go beyond just using your name, though. They may use a photo of you to prove identity. Or worse, they may take your photos or videos and use them to create new photos or videos of you. Often these images show you doing something you would never normally do or meeting with people you'd never normally be with.

Causing Damage

One of the biggest problems with identity theft and deepfakes is using a person's image to create sexually explicit images—just like they did with the singer Taylor Swift (see page 10). These images are known as nonconsensual intimate images (NCII). Although there are laws against NCII, the damage they cause to a person's reputation may never be mended.

Finding out that you have been a victim of identity theft is scary. This is especially true when your photos are used to cause you harm.

Bullying with Deepfakes

Deepfakes can also be used in cyberbullying. Cyberbullying is the use of online technology to threaten, upset, embarrass, or target another person. It's bullying in the online world. Cyberbullying can happen on any device with an Internet connection. Using deepfake technology, a person could create very convincing videos or audio clips to spread false information about a person or put them in a bad light.

When the person realizes that such images or videos exist, they are then blackmailed. That means the creator of the images asks for money to remove them. The problem is that once things are online, it's very difficult to remove them completely. For example, someone may have taken a screenshot or saved the video. That then means even if the image is removed from the place where it was originally posted, it still exists somewhere else, and can still be used.

Creating explicit deepfakes is a very real and very scary part of identity theft. A 2023 study into deepfakes found that explicit images make up a staggering 98 percent of all the online deepfake videos. The study also found that 99 percent of the victims were women.

You've Been Scammed!

There are millions of scammers operating in the world, and many of them are online. The Internet offers scammers anonymity. That means they remain unknown. Safe behind a computer screen, their identity is never revealed. So, they can create deepfakes to trick innocent people.

Scammers most often use deepfakes to get money. For example, criminals may take a small snippet of a person's voice. They then use this to create an audio clip of the "victim" asking for money. This is sent to the person's friends and family. Because no one wants to see their loved ones in difficulty, the money is paid. A recent survey suggested that 1 in 10 people have received messages like this. More than 75 percent of them lost money to such scams.

It's easier than you think to be caught out by a scam.

Cyberbullying can leave you feeling anxious and depressed. It may seem difficult, but always try to talk to a trusted adult. They can help you deal with the situation.

Hit Hard by Deepfakes

Deepfakes created for education and entertainment can be great. Any tech that helps students has to be a good thing. However, the more sinister side of deepfakes can cause long-lasting damage to the victims. If an image of yourself is used in a video without your consent, this can cause deep upset.

The Emotional Effect

People whose images have been used in deepfake videos often feel really embarrassed or anxious, and experience severe stress. These feelings may last a long time and could lead to depression. There have been instances where teens have committed suicide, or killed themselves, because of cyberbullying. If you are being cyberbullied with deepfake imagery, it's really important to get help. In the next chapter, we will look at what you can do if you find out that you are in a deepfake.

Damaging Relationships

If family members and friends see their relative and friend doing unusual things in deepfake videos, this could lead to problems within these relationships. Even if it's not the person's fault, the trust may be broken. That can then make a relationship difficult to repair.

Damaging Reputations

As an adult in the working world, a deepfake can lead to a person being suspended from work or losing their job. For example, in one deepfake, a teacher was called into the school head's office after a video of her shouting insults at a student went viral. The teacher was suspended while the school carried out an investigation. Although the video was found to be fake and the teacher went back to work, her reputation had been harmed and she had suffered a lot of stress.

The Power of Words and Images

Hearing the words of politicians, public figures, and celebrities has a huge impact on society. That is especially dangerous when they are words those people never said, but are instead fake. Not everyone is familiar with tech, and many people will instantly believe what they are shown. That is particularly true in a time of uncertainty or emergency. When this happens, mass panic can break out.

The power of political deepfake imagery was revealed in 2023, when an image of an explosion near the Pentagon caused terror. Who had bombed the Pentagon? Was this just the first of several bomb blasts? The image was picked up by news agencies around the world and the bomb blast made headlines everywhere. This had an effect on the US stock market because people feared for their investments. Eventually, the Arlington County Fire Department issued a statement explaining that there was no explosion or incident. The image was a deepfake.

The Pentagon is the headquarters of the United States Department of Defense (DoD). Any problem with security at the Pentagon is likely to cause panic and fear in the country.

UNDERSTANDING DEEPFAKES

In this chapter we looked at how deepfakes can be used. For some, it may have been interesting to see that deepfake tech can be used to do good. However, for many, the negatives can be quite scary. Let's recap the good and bad of deepfake tech.

1 Education Can Be Brought to Life

Using deepfake tech, classrooms can become a space for fun learning. Historical figures can today be brought to life in an entirely new and fascinating way. Lessons can also be shaped to each student's needs.

2 The Tech Can Help Doctors

Advancements in deepfake tech mean that machines such as MRI scanners can be improved. That makes them more efficient at discovering problems, such as tumors.

3 Deepfakes Can Lead to Doubt

Deepfakes in the media that are used to spread disinformation can lead to a general feeling of mistrust and doubt. People don't know what to believe.

4 There Can Be Consequences

Deepfake technology has a sinister side when it is used in identity theft, scams, or to bully someone. The victims not only suffer emotionally and may struggle with anxiety and stress, but their relationships and careers could suffer too.

Trust Is Key

In any relationship, trust is important. When there is trust, your relationship is healthier and you have a sense of well-being. However, when it comes to the digital world, blind trust can be a problem. Blind trust is when a person believes anything and everything they are told without question or doubt. Blind trust leads to people believing and spreading fake news. When it comes to news, you might think that it is believable. But always think twice about what you see and hear.

CHAPTER 3

Spotting a Deepfake

Some deepfakes are easy to spot. For example, a yellow dog is not seen in nature and neither is a polka-dot cat! Some creators are very proud of their work, so they label it as a deepfake. And don't forget in some countries, the law says that you have to label a deepfake. But would you be able to spot one? In a recent survey only 57 percent of people surveyed believed that they could tell the difference between real images or deepfakes. The problem is that as software advances and people get better at using it, spotting a deepfake is going to become more difficult.

As software advances, it will be easier to create deepfakes but possibly more difficult to spot them.

Looking for a Fake Image

Face swapping is one of the simplest ways to create a deepfake. In a face swap, one face is superimposed onto another. In a poor-quality face swap, the new image may look a little odd. That is especially the case around the area where the new face has been blended with the original forehead. The color, texture, and hairline (where the skin on a forehead ends and the hair begins) often quickly give away the fake.

Telltale Signs

In a more sophisticated image, you need to look a little more closely to spot giveaways such as eyes that are different sizes or earrings that don't match. In the image of Pope Francis in his puffer jacket (see page 9), the chain his crucifix hung from had missing links. To spot a fake, try to pay attention to the teeth and skin of a person. Do they look real? Are there too many teeth—individual teeth are hard to generate. Is the skin just too perfect?

Look at reflections and shadows too. Are they accurate or are there weird reflections that don't match the objects in the image?

Try a Reverse Search

Sometimes after checking out an image, you may be undecided about whether an image is real or fake. If in doubt, double check by doing a reverse image search. There are apps that help you do this. A free reverse image search is also available through Google. It's called Search by Image.

To use Search by Image, all you need to do is drag and drop or upload your image. Google then searches the Web to find related images. Related means the exact image, a similar image, or a mix of images in which the original image has been used. This can help you find the source of the image. A reverse search can also help you discover where else the image has been used, for example, on which websites. If the image has been changed in any way, that will show up too, helping you spot the fake.

The Mona Lisa is a very famous painting, but is this photo of it real or a fake? A reverse search would tell you that it's an AI-generated image and not a photo of the real painting.

In 2019, a global survey showed that only 13 percent of people knew what a deepfake was. By 2022, this number had more than doubled to 29 percent. That may sound like progress has been made. On the other hand, it's concerning that 71 percent of people surveyed don't know what deepfakes are. Not knowing what deepfakes are means being unable to spot them. Even worse, it may mean believing everything that is seen and heard, real or not.

Sound engineers spend time making sure the video and audio tracks match up. Deepfake creators may miss this and the sound and audio may not be synchronized.

Look at the Image

When trying to spot the difference between a real or fake video, start by paying careful attention to all of the things you would notice in an image. That includes the hair, skin, teeth, jewelry, and shadows. Then start to look at the video more closely. One of the biggest giveaways is blinking. The average person blinks 15 to 20 times each minute. Watch and count. Is the person blinking too little or too much? Now you should look at the edge of the face. Is there suspicious flickering around it?

Study the Sound

Audio, or sound, is the next thing to focus on. First, check if the facial expressions match the audio. Facial expressions are how a face moves to show emotions. Do the facial expressions you see match what you're hearing? (Pay careful attention to the eyebrows, which can give away a lot.) What about the tone of voice—does it suit the person? For example, a man with bulging biceps would seldom have a high-pitched squeaky voice. The audio should also be synchronized to the image. This means the person's lips are moving to make the same sounds you are hearing.

#SpotTheFake

Sometimes, videomakers use a cryptographic algorithm to show that their videos are legitimate. A cryptographic algorithm is a mathematical formula that scrambles, or mixes up, data to make it unreadable. It is used to keep information secure and private. Videomakers can also insert hashtags throughout a video. If the hashtags suddenly change, the video could be a deepfake.

Slow It Down

If you're still not sure if a video is real or fake, don't just look at it on your phone. Instead, try watching it on a computer or other device with a large screen. As you watch the video, slow it down. Now zoom in and pay careful attention to the person's lips. Are they moving in keeping with the words? In a real video, the audio will always be synchronized.

Watching a video on a screen bigger than a phone screen will often help you decide if the video is real or fake.

A Mini Fact-Check

If you think something may be fake, but are not sure, it's better to check the facts. This doesn't mean spending hours searching online to see what you can find. Start with simple things, such as the weather. Is the weather shown in the image correct? Does it match the video or the image's time stamp? If the video is dated as July, why are people wearing hats and gloves?

Clues in Location

Next, ask yourself if the geography makes sense. If the image is intending to show a city in the United States, does the city "look" American? For example, what color are the cabs? What language can you see in signs? Then ask yourself if what you're seeing is possible or likely. Are there background noises that don't match the rest of the video? For example, if the video shows the countryside and you hear city noises, you know it is a fake.

Sift Through

If you're still not sure after your basic fact-check, take your detective work one step further with the SIFT Method. The SIFT Method was developed by Mike Caulfield, a research scientist at the University of Washington. Caulfield has taught thousands of people how to spot disinformation using the SIFT Method. It works like this:

- **Stop**—before you read or share information, always pause. Headlines are designed to get clicks so think about the headline, what does it mean to you? What do you already know about the topic?
- **Investigate** the source. What is the source of the image—where does it come from? Is the source reliable? Is it credible? See what you can find about the source— not just from the website but from reviews and what others are saying.

In 2020, a video of the late Queen Elizabeth II of England dancing and giving a speech about the power of technology went viral. At the time, she was 94 years old. Is it really likely that a lady of her age, and a queen, would behave in this way?

A simple fact-check will tell you that this is a deepfake and former President Joe Biden was not arrested.

- **Find** better coverage. Do some research—what do others say? See what factcheckers have to say.
- **Trace** claims, quotes, and media to their source. Try to find the original source of information. Remember that people "twist" the facts to suit their own needs, for example, cutting out parts of an interview could take someone's words out of context and lead you to believe something that's not true.

STUDIES IN ONLINE SURVIVAL

A recent survey confirmed that only 22 percent of students feel confident in their ability to spot a deepfake. Interestingly, another survey found that people can accurately tell a fake only 24.5 percent of the time. So while people may be confident in their ability to spot fakes, they may not actually be able to do so!

Trust Yourself

You may have heard the saying "always trust your gut." This means to trust what the voice inside you is saying. Trusting your gut is really important when it comes to figuring out if something is a fake. If you feel that something is not right or makes you feel uncomfortable, it probably isn't right and you should approach with caution.

Talk It Through

If you aren't sure if something is genuine or not, speak up rather than keep quiet. By voicing your concerns, you could help stop fake news spreading or someone falling for a scam. Sometimes, you may be too close to something. This means you've seen something similar before so you don't pick up on things you might otherwise spot. For this reason, if you've seen something a few times and aren't convinced if it's genuine or fake, ask a friend or trusted adult for their opinion. Because they will be looking at things for the first time, they are more likely to spot problems and make you more aware of things.

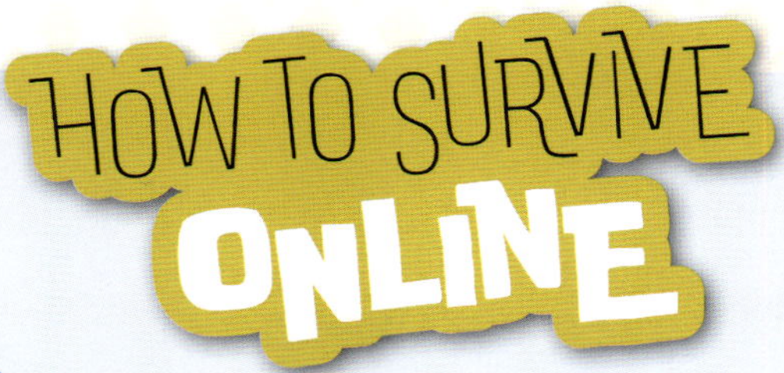

When "Fact" Is Fiction

It is really difficult not to be affected by upsetting images shared with you online. But just as with all other types of information, you need to question the validity, or truth, of each image before reacting to it. For example, you might be sent an image of a little girl. She may look dirty, have torn clothes, and be surrounded by rubble. At the bottom of the image is a number to send money to help children in war-torn Gaza. It can be very tempting to immediately call the number and hand over money. But do you really know who that money is going to? Before you commit to any message like this, always do your homework and apply the SIFT method:

- **Stop!**
- **Investigate** the source: Are you sure the information is genuine?
- **Find** better coverage: Always fact-check the information carefully.
- **Trace**: Try to go back to the original source of information—has it been changed or manipulated?

Along with applying the SIFT method, check with your parents or a trusted adult, such as a teacher.

UNDERSTANDING DEEPFAKES

It's impossible to spot a fake every time and you will not always get it right. However, if you at least know what to look for, you're on track to spotting a deepfake. Let's revisit what we've learned about spotting deepfakes.

1 Face Swaps Can Be Easier to Identify

If the forehead or hair line of the image looks a bit odd, you're likely looking at a deepfake. Look at the eyes too—are there strange reflections in them or is one bigger than the other?

2 Audio Should Match Up

The audio should match the lip movements of the person speaking. If not, it's a deepfake.

3 The SIFT Method Can Help

Before you repost an image or part with your money, apply the SIFT Method to check it's real: **Stop**, **Identify** the source, **Find** better coverage, **Trace** claims.

4 Trust Your Gut

If something feels a little off, it probably is.

It Pays to Be Suspicious

There's no shame in being overly cautious and suspicious of things. Always try to figure out if something is actually real rather than be duped by a deepfake. In the next chapter, we'll look at what to do if you are in a deepfake.

Protecting Yourself

In the real world, you always try your best to keep your belongings safe from criminals. You probably make sure your phone and computer are securely stored. The front door of your house is closed and locked when you go out and about and when you go to bed at night. In the same way, you need to protect yourself in the online world.

Danger Online

In the online world, you have to protect yourself from cybercriminals. These are criminals whose goal is to steal your passwords, data, and identity. They then create scams. By protecting yourself from cybercrimes, you are also protecting yourself from becoming the victim of a deepfake.

Protecting with Passwords

One of the simplest ways to protect yourself is to set passwords to access your devices and apps. These need to be passwords that are difficult for others to guess. Do not use your date of birth or your name, even your mom's maiden name is a no-go. In a survey, it was found that three in five Americans use their birthdays or names as their passwords. Make sure you have different passwords for different apps.

Keep your passwords to yourself and make sure no one can see you entering your passwords.

Take care when working in a public place that offers free Wi-Fi, such as a library or café. There, you are more vulnerable to cybercrime than if you work on a secure network.

Although it can be annoying and difficult to remember different passwords, it's safer than having one. To create a strong password, use a combination of letters, numbers, and special characters such as #, %, or @.

Other Checks for Safety

Once you have set up strong passwords, try to use multifactor authentication or two-factor authentication. This is an extra level of protection and includes things such as a biometric face scan, finger print scan, and code sent to your phone. This may make logging in a longer process but again, it's safer and well worth investing the time to do so.

STUDIES IN ONLINE SURVIVAL

Passwords help guard all your personal data. They can be the difference between keeping safe and becoming a victim of a deepfake. Although people know what they should be doing to stay safe, very few actually do it. For example, *Cybernews*, a cybersecurity publication, analyzed 15 billion passwords found in public data breaches. The research showed that the most common password used was 123456. In second place was 123456789. A survey of more than 3,000 adults in the United States found the following:

- Only 37 percent used two-factor authentication
- 36 percent kept track of their passwords on paper
- Only 34 percent regularly changed their passwords.

It Pays to Be Private

Once your devices are secure, you need to also operate safely online, especially on social media. If you have your own social media accounts, make sure they are set to private. The fewer people who can see your content, the better. In an ideal world, the number one way to stay safe would be not to share anything online. However, in today's world, that is difficult to do, so chose carefully when it comes to followers. If you don't know someone in real life, don't let them follow you in the cyberworld.

Stop Before You Share

If you share your images to an online platform, share only to your friends. Don't share with the general public. Better yet, share to only a few people. This means if there is a breach, it's easier to find out who shared the image. Do not share images of other people without their permission. This is especially true for younger brothers and sisters. Do not share images of yourself you may later regret.

Sharing online is part of being a teenager today. But remember, the more you share, the easier you are to target.

Think Before You Click

Be cautious when you receive emails, messages, texts, or other digital communication. This is especially true if you're told to "act fast" or "don't delay." Deepfake creators will often try to work on your emotions so that you download malware. That gives them access to your devices without you realizing it. Their other goal is to make you share personal information.

How to Share Safely

Online sharing platforms have made teamwork and group projects much easier. You can do your project at home while your friend does the same. But what happens if one team member has an image or video that someone needs urgently and isn't around to upload it? While it may be tempting to message your friend your log-in details so they can access your work, this is really not a good idea because:

- You may trust your friend. However, imagine they work from a mall, for example, where there's free Wi-Fi. That will mean your data is not secure and could be accessed by others.
- If your friend's phone is lost or stolen, whoever finds it has your details too. They can then use both your data however they like.
- Your friend may not realize the danger of sharing your information. They may decide to have a little fun and create content using other images, videos, or reels stored on your phone.

To avoid all these situations, create a folder on a file-sharing platform. There, everyone working on the project can add relevant images as well as audio and video clips. That way, only those with the link have access to the images and only those images, not all of the images you have on your device.

Help! I've Found a Deepfake!

At some point—and because you have newfound fake-spotting skills—you will come across a deepfake. How you deal with the fakes can make all the difference to you and others around you. Some social media sites have officially banned the use of malicious deepfakes. These sites have a platform on which to report the fake—usually just by checking a drop-down box. If you know something is a fake and you've reported it, never share it. Encourage others not to share either.

Help! I'm in a Deepfake!

It's one thing to be able to identify a deepfake when one appears on your screen, but what do you do when it's a deepfake and you're in it? It's important not to panic in this instance. Instead, work through these steps one by one:

1. Tell someone what has happened. Try talking to a trusted adult such as a parent, teacher, or school counselor.
2. Report the deepfake, just as you would any other deepfake.
3. Take screenshots as evidence, noting the URLs.

Some deepfakes are very funny and will keep you and your friends laughing. Others can be hurtful, so think twice before you share.

Teen Need to Know

In 2023, a 14-year-old girl named Francesca Mani was called into her school's vice principal's office. The vice principal told Mani that she and other girls at her school had been targeted in deepfake images. The content creator had used an app to create naked images of the girls, and then circulated the images. Mani decided rather than keep quiet, she'd take action. She went public and took her fight to lawmakers and media outlets to raise awareness. She has also set up a website and charity to help other victims of deepfakes.

4. Record or screenshot any interactions you have with the content creator if you have contact.

5. Contact the platform's support team and explain what has happened, asking them to remove the fake.

6. As you know, there are laws around deepfake creation so reporting the fake to the authorities and seeking legal counsel are steps in the right direction. The Cyber Civil Rights Initiative can also help in these situations. It offers legal help and support for people affected by nonconsensual explicit images.

7. There are also organizations that can help: STOPNCII.org and TakeItDown are platforms that help to remove nonconsensual intimate images.

If your image has been in a deepfake, ask for help with managing the situation.

Deepfake Detectives

While there are organizations that can help you take down deepfakes, others have been set up to help you detect a deepfake before it has time to cause you harm. These companies have developed deepfake detection tools. Deepfake detection tools use various methods to study digital content and figure out if it's been created by AI. Interestingly, many of them use AI to do this. Through deep learning, they aim to identify fake media without needing to compare it to the original or unaltered media.

Searching for Deepfakes

One of the top detection tools is called Sensity. Sensity monitors users in real-time. It is able to detect face swaps, manipulated audio, and AI-generated images. The creators of Sensity claim it has an 98 percent accuracy in detecting deepfakes. They claim that other tools that don't use AI have only a 70 percent accuracy rate. Sensity also has training materials to help people learn more about deepfakes in order to improve their detection skills.

Deepfake detection software is like a detective working to solve a crime. Tech companies are working hard to stay one step ahead of deepfake creators.

In the working world, people can lose their jobs as a result of a deepfake scam or from being in a deepfake.

Truth-Seeking Tools

While some technology aims to detect deepfakes, authentication software is also used to prove that something is genuine. As you've read, Google has a reverse image search. It also has tools to track the use of your name and likeness. Through the Google platform, users can access text-to-speech conversion tools to verify speakers. This helps ensure audio clips are genuine. Similarly, Microsoft has a video AI authenticator. This is a free tool that gives images and videos a score for how likely they are to have been manipulated.

Teen Need to Know

From the moment a deepfake is viewed, disinformation can be spread. When something is thought to be a fake, it can take time to prove that it is. And even then, there may be people who still believe the fake to be true.

In April 2024, a high school principal in Maryland fell victim to a deepfake attack. An athletic director faked a recording of the principal making racist remarks. The athletic director hoped to get the principal fired. Although the audio clip was proven to be a fake, many people still believed it to be genuine. By using early detection and authentication tools, this situation and the harm it caused could have been avoided.

UNDERSTANDING DEEPFAKES

You've reached the end of the book and now know what to do if you come across a deepfake. You also know what to do if images of you are used to create a deepfake. Here is one last overview.

1 Keep Devices and Data Safe

You wouldn't invite robbers into your home, so don't give cybercriminals an opportunity to access your devices and data. Always use strong passwords and two-step authentication to keep safe. Do not share your passwords with anyone.

2 Think Before Sharing

It may be tempting to gather as many followers as possible, but try to be selective about who you allow to follow you. Avoid oversharing content, especially images and videos of yourself.

3 You Can Fight Back If You Are a Victim

It is really upsetting to learn that you are the subject of a deepfake. But if this happens, don't panic. Instead, tell a trusted adult, collect evidence, ask the sites to remove the fake. Seek legal action if necessary.

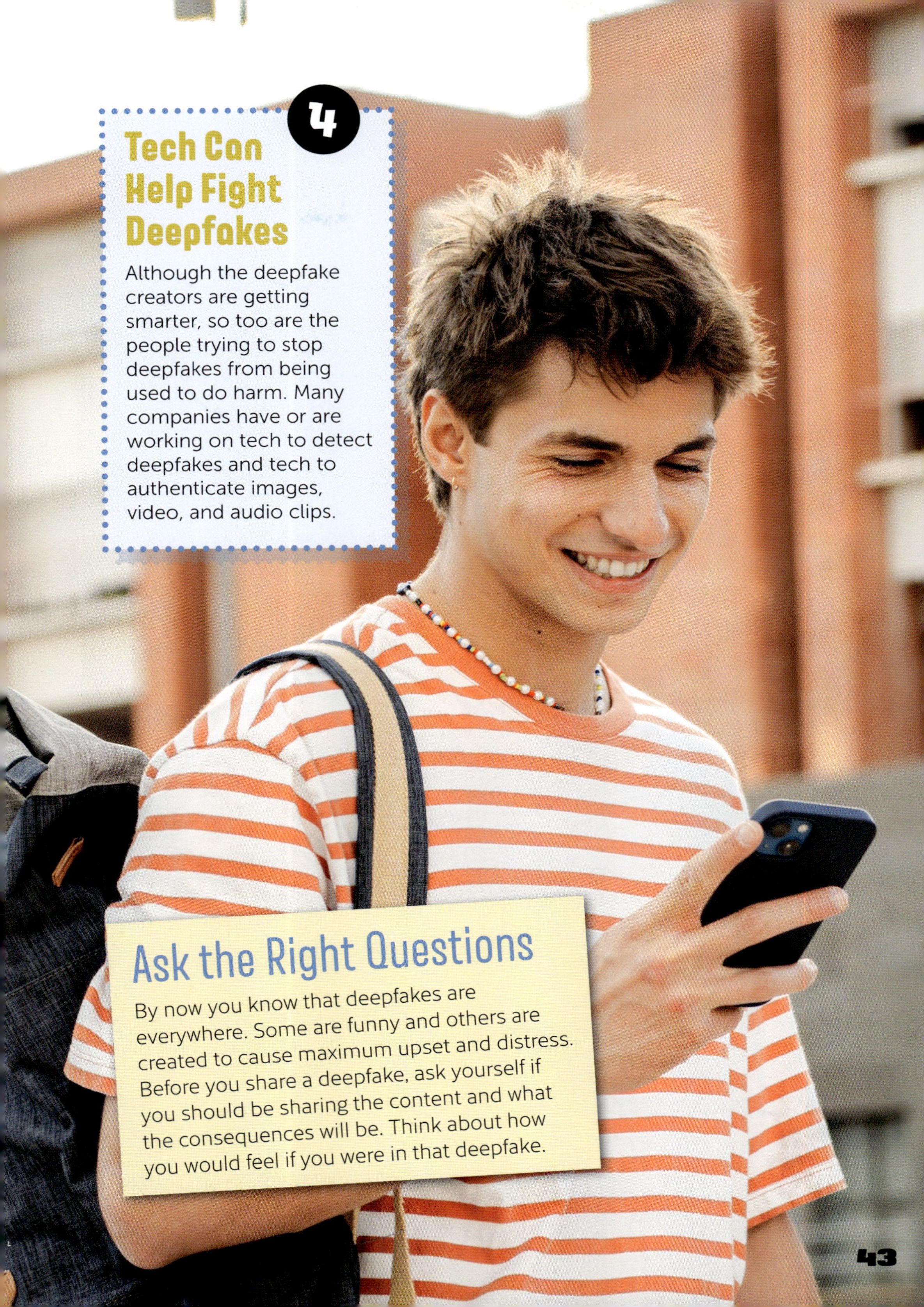

4 Tech Can Help Fight Deepfakes

Although the deepfake creators are getting smarter, so too are the people trying to stop deepfakes from being used to do harm. Many companies have or are working on tech to detect deepfakes and tech to authenticate images, video, and audio clips.

Ask the Right Questions

By now you know that deepfakes are everywhere. Some are funny and others are created to cause maximum upset and distress. Before you share a deepfake, ask yourself if you should be sharing the content and what the consequences will be. Think about how you would feel if you were in that deepfake.

Be a Responsible Digital Citizen

Around the world, there are billions of Internet users. They are called digital citizens. Each and every person accessing the Internet should aim to act responsibly when online. By being a responsible digital citizen, you will keep yourself and others safe from the dangers of the Internet, and especially from deepfakes.

Keep Yourself and Others Safe

To be a responsible digital citizen, you need to protect yourself, friends, and family online. Remember to create strong passwords and don't give them to anyone. Anyone with access to your devices and apps can create a deepfake using your images or video content. Protecting yourself and others also includes keeping your personal information private. Never share personal information such as your name, address, and name of your school.

Show Respect

As a teenager, you're learning and growing as a person all the time. You're also finding your own set of beliefs. Be responsible by behaving properly online. This includes asking permission before sharing photos online. It also means not creating images of others without their permission.

On average, today's teens spend around 7 hours a day in front of screens. Use your screentime to be constructive.

Be a responsible digital citizen
and stay safe by not oversharing.

If you find a deepfake that uses a friend or classmate, as difficult as
it may be, let them know. Tell them privately as soon as possible.
Always take action—don't just wait for someone else to do it.

Be Kind

Deepfakes can be a source of entertainment. Funny reels that
are obviously fake and not malicious can really make us smile.
However, people's image or likeness can also be used in deepfakes
to cause them harm. Never share a malicious deepfake. Before you
reshare any posts, stop and think about the consequences of your
actions. Is what you're sharing acceptable, kind, and positive?

Be Cautious

The Internet can bombard us with facts, figures, videos, and
images. As we now know, not everything you see and read is true.
Being a responsible digital citizen means not trusting everything
you read or see online. Before you post something or comment
on it, think carefully about the content you're sharing.

STUDIES IN ONLINE SURVIVAL

Part of being a responsible digital citizen involves being
smart about disinformation, and not sharing it. A recent
survey found that fake news, lies, or rumors often spread
faster than truthful news. In one study, the top 1 percent of
rumors found on X reached 1,000 to 100,000 people, while
truthful news rarely reached more than 1,000 people.

Glossary

accessible easy to use

algorithms a process or set of rules that is followed in problem-solving

anxiety a mental health problem in which people may experience mild or intensely worrying thoughts and feelings that are difficult to manage

artificial intelligence (AI) a computer system that can perform tasks that normally only a human brain could carry out

character the qualities that make a person who they are

crucifix a cross with a figure of Jesus Christ on it

deception hiding the truth

defame to say bad or untrue things about someone

depression a mental health problem in which people may experience intense feelings of sadness, generally feeling low, or having a lack of interest in anything

distracting affecting someone's ability to pay attention

doctored changed, often to trick or deceive people

explicit relating to sex

fraudulent false and dishonest

generative adversarial network (GAN) a computer network that trains two different networks to compete against each other

identity characteristics or information that identify who a person is

insights the thoughts, actions, and motivation behind something

interact communicate with and have an effect on other people

justice the legal system of a country

magnetic resonance imaging (MRI) scans detailed pictures of the inside of people's bodies. They are created by machines that use radio waves, magnets, and computers

maiden name a woman's surname before she was married and took her husband's surname

manipulate to change something for your own advantage or benefit

memory card a card that contains computer memory and is used in digital devices to store data

networks systems of computers and devices that are connected and operate together

predictions things that people believe or say will happen

reputation what people think about someone

retrieves takes back

scam a fraudulent scheme

service providers companies that allow people access to the Internet

sinister evil or harmful

source where something started

superimposed put on top of

suspended made to leave a job for a period of time

tumors masses of tissue that sometimes grow in a person's body

unverified not confirmed, substantiated, or proven to be true

URLs the abbreviation for Uniform Resource Locators: the addresses that show where pages can be found on the World Wide Web

values a person's moral principles and beliefs

Find Out More

BOOKS

Brezina, Carona. *Artificial Intelligence and You* (The Promise and Perils of Technology). Rosen Publishing Group, 2020.

Delisle, Raina. *Breaking News: Why Media Matters* (Orca Think 10). Orca Book Publishers, 2023.

Kuel, Ashley. *Deepfakes* (In the News: Need to Know Set Two). Silvertip Books, 2025.

Scientific American Editors. *Artificial Intelligence* (Scientific American Explores Big Ideas). Scientific American, 2023.

WEBSITES

Test yourself and your friends to see if you can spot whether these are deepfakes or real images:
https://detectfakes.kellogg.northwestern.edu

If you are not sure if something is true or not, check the facts at:
www.factcheck.org

There are some top tips for teens to stay safe online at:
https://kidshealth.org/en/teens/internet-safety.html

Learn more about deepfakes and how to spot them at:
www.teenvogue.com/story/what-is-deepfake

Publisher's note to educators and parents:
All the websites featured above have been carefully reviewed to ensure that they are suitable for students. However, many websites change often, and we cannot guarantee that a site's future contents will continue to meet our high standards of educational value. Please be advised that students should be closely monitored whenever they access the Internet.

Index

About the Author

Jennifer Sanderson has written books on many different topics, from tennis and baby animals to geography and self-care. She has two teenagers who, like all young people, are learning to navigate the digital world. She's hoping this book will give them and other readers the skills they need to enjoy the online world safely.